CONTENTS

Rubbish and Waste

Everyone throws out rubbish. You and your family probably fill several bags a week with waste paper, empty cans, plastic bottles and glass jars, food scraps, and other rubbish.

In a market street, empty cardboard and wooden boxes have been piled high, ready to be taken away by refuse, or waste, collectors.

Recycling

HODDER
Wayland

an imprint of Hodder Children's Books

Environment Starts Here!
Recycling

OTHER TITLES IN THE SERIES
Water · Food · Transport

Produced for Wayland Publishers Limited by
Lionheart Books
10, Chelmsford Square
London NW10 3AR
England

Designer: Ben White
Editor: Lionel Bender
Picture Research: Madeleine Samuel
Electronic make-up: Mike Pilley, Radius
Illustrated by Rudi Visi

First Published in 1998 by Wayland (Publishers) Limited
Reprinted in 2001 by Hodder Wayland,
an imprint of Hodder Children's Books

British Library Cataloguing in Publication Data
Royston, Angela
Recycling. - (Environment starts here! ; 3)
1. Recycling (Waste, etc.) - Juvenile literature
I. Title
363.7'282
ISBN 0 7502 3426 1

Printed and bound in Hong Kong

Picture Acknowledgements
Pages 1: Ecoscene/Nick Hawkes. 4: Eye Ubiquitous/Craig Hutchins. 7: Wayland Picture
Library. 9. Ecoscene/Lorenzo Lees. 10: Ecoscene/Ian Harwood. 11: Britstock/IFA-Bernard
Ducke. 12: Eye Ubiquitous/Steve Miller. 14: Zefa/Stockmarket. 15: Ecoscene/Kevin King.
16: Zefa/Stockmarket. 17: Britstock/IFA-Hans Jurgen Wiedl. 18: Eye Ubiquitous/Jim Winkley.
19: Ecoscene/Towse. 20: Ecoscene/Sally Morgan. 21: Eye Ubiquitous/Paul Seheult. 21(inset):
Ecoscene/Sally Morgan. 22: Wayland/Angus Blackburn. 23, 24, 25, 26: Zefa/Stockmarket.
27: Ecoscene/Rob Nichol. 28: Ecoscene/Stuart Donachie. 29: Zefa/Stockmarket.
Cover: Zefa/Stockmarket.

The photo on page 1 shows children putting newspapers into a paper recycling container.

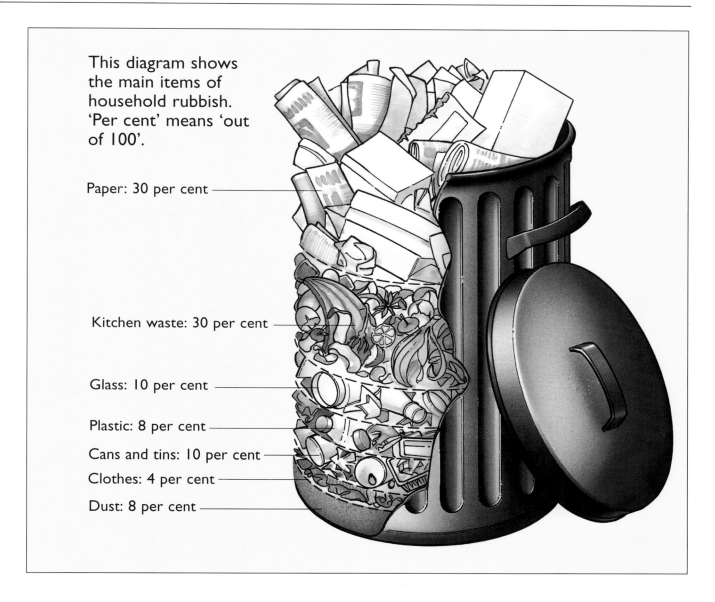

This diagram shows the main items of household rubbish. 'Per cent' means 'out of 100'.

Paper: 30 per cent

Kitchen waste: 30 per cent

Glass: 10 per cent

Plastic: 8 per cent

Cans and tins: 10 per cent

Clothes: 4 per cent

Dust: 8 per cent

Your school probably has several bins that fill up with paper, broken toys, old pens, and so on. Over a year most families throw away between one and two tonnes of rubbish. That's the weight of an Indian elephant!

Packaging Material

Most of the rubbish in your dustbin is packaging from food and other goods. Food from the supermarket is often packaged in a can, plastic bag or cardboard box, or wrapped in cellophane paper.

The contents of a shopping bag shows a huge variety of packaging materials.

Paper bag

Plastic bottle

Cardboard box

Glass jar

String bag

Steel can

Aluminium drink can

Plastic tub

Plastic tub

Cardboard tray and cellulose film

Packaging keeps the food clean and protects it from being damaged. Packaging makes things look attractive and exciting, and it may give information, like instructions, too.

A boy and girl empty and sort through the contents of a waste bin. Most of the waste is food packaging material.

7

Needless Waste

Sometimes too much packaging is used. Computer games and toys often come in a large box, with cardboard sections and advertising leaflets inside. This can make you think you are getting more for your money.

A girl unpacks the shopping to throw away the unwanted packaging.

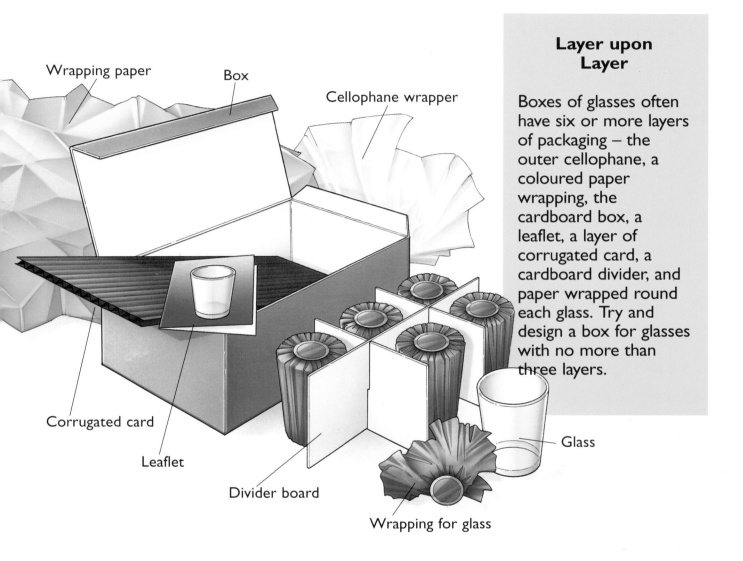

Wrapping paper

Box

Cellophane wrapper

Corrugated card

Leaflet

Divider board

Wrapping for glass

Glass

Layer upon Layer

Boxes of glasses often have six or more layers of packaging – the outer cellophane, a coloured paper wrapping, the cardboard box, a leaflet, a layer of corrugated card, a cardboard divider, and paper wrapped round each glass. Try and design a box for glasses with no more than three layers.

Most shops and supermarkets give every customer a plastic carrier bag to take their shopping home, whether they need it or not. Although plastic bags and boxes can be used again, most people get a new one each time.

Bury it or Burn it?

We produce so much rubbish that getting rid of it brings problems. Some rubbish is burned in huge incinerators. Smoke from incinerators pollutes, or dirties, the air.

Most rubbish is squashed flat and tipped into huge holes in the ground called landfill sites. As the rubbish rots, it produces poisons. These can sometimes pollute nearby rivers and streams.

A bulldozer is used to flatten a pile of household rubbish dumped on a landfill site.

Dustbin lorries drive into an incineration plant to deliver their loads for burning.

Private Fahrzeuge

Städtische Fahrzeuge ↑

11

A mechanical grab is used to sort through a pile of scrap metal from cars, refrigerators and household machines.

What is Recycling?

Much rubbish can be recycled instead of being thrown away. Recycling means using materials again to make something new. First, the materials have to be sorted and separated into groups.

Empty glass jars can be washed and crushed. The glass can be recycled to make bottles. Paper, metal cans, plastics and car oil can all be recycled, sometimes many times.

Household items that can be recycled. The shoes and clothes could be recycled into new materials, or just reused by another person.

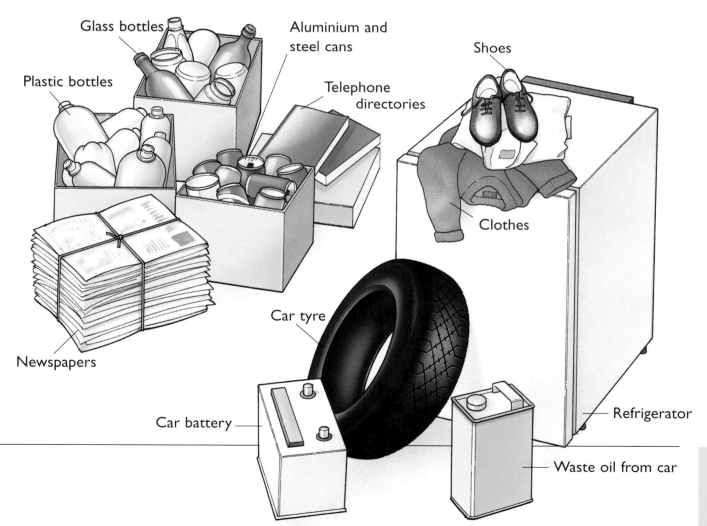

Glass bottles

Aluminium and steel cans

Plastic bottles

Telephone directories

Shoes

Clothes

Newspapers

Car tyre

Car battery

Refrigerator

Waste oil from car

Why Recycle?

When you put aside everything that can be recycled, there is less rubbish left to be buried or burned. This means less pollution from landfill sites and incinerators.

Recycling uses less of the Earth's supply of resources or useful materials. For example, fewer trees are cut down when paper is recycled. This is because paper is usually made from trees.

Computers are made with expensive and rare metals and other materials that can be recycled. The plastic casing can also be reused.

Kitchen waste is piled on top of dead leaves to make compost. Compost is rotting vegetable matter that is recycled to fertilize growing plants.

Trees are cut from a forest to make wood pulp for paper. The huge logs have to be carried by truck to the papermill.

Saving Energy

Making something from recycled materials uses less energy than making it from new materials. Most energy comes from coal, oil or gas, which are running out.

Recycling saves work as well as energy. Digging metals out of the ground and chopping down trees is not only difficult. It also uses petrol for machines and electricity.

Sheets of steel being made from hot, molten iron. Coal must be burned to melt the iron. It is much easier and cheaper to make recycled steel.

Sorting and Separating

Materials that are going to be recycled must be sorted into different groups, such as paper, metal, glass and plastic. The sorting starts when you put each kind of material into a different bag.

These recycling bins are lined up outside a supermarket in the USA. The bins are marked for different types of materials.

Recycling Bins

Find out how recycling is organized in your area.
Are there special bins at the supermarket for bottles or paper?
Do you have to do anything to bottles or cans before you send them to be recycled?

Household waste is sorted by hand at a recycling centre.

Bags of recyclable items may be picked up from your home by collectors, or you may have to take them to a recycling centre.

At a recycling centre, cardboard, paper, steel and aluminium cans are separated. Glass is sorted into clear, green and brown.

New from Old

New paper is made by chopping and mashing wood into tiny pieces and then mixing it to a pulp with water. Old paper that is recycled simply has to be mixed with water to make new pulp.

All kinds of paper can be made from recycled pulp, even good quality writing paper. Look for the 'recycled' sign on kitchen rolls, toilet rolls and on cardboard and paper packaging.

At a recycling centre in Jakarta, Indonesia, unwanted metal containers and boxes are broken up into flat sheets.

Main photo: Waste paper is collected for recycling.

Inset photo: After the paper has been mashed into a pulp, it is rolled into flat sheets to be used again.

Bottles and Cans

Some companies sell drinks in returnable glass bottles which are collected, washed and used again. Reusing glass bottles uses less energy than crushing and melting old bottles to make new glass.

Children sort empty glass bottles by colour then load them into recycling bins.

In Malawi, watering cans made from recycled scrap metal are put on display for sale to local people.

Magnetic Sorter

Use a magnet to test whether a can is made of steel or aluminium. The magnet will stick to a steel can, but not to an aluminium one. Aluminium is more valuable than steel so make sure you recycle it.

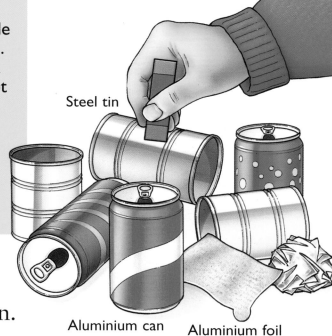

Steel tin

Aluminium can Aluminium foil

Most drinks cans and tins are made of steel which can be recycled again and again. An empty can of beans could end up as a spoon, or as part of a car or as paperclips!

The fleecy jacket and hat worn by this mountaineer are filled with fibres made from recycled plastic. The fibres trap body heat, keeping the mountaineer warm.

Recycling Plastic

Plastic is cheap to make, tough and long lasting. It is so long lasting, it does not rot away when it is buried in landfill sites.

Some kinds of plastic can be recycled more easily than others. Soft drinks bottles are melted and made into plastic pipes, floor tiles, and even into trousers and anoraks.

Poisonous plastics and liquids such as paints and oils are being collected to make them safe before recycling them.

Reuse

Lots of people throw away things that could be reused. Unwanted clothes, books, toys and other things may not be recycled easily. But they could be used by someone else.

Car boot sales, jumble sales and school fairs all make money by selling things that can be reused. Many charity shops raise money to help people or animals by selling second-hand things for reuse.

Household antiques on display for sale and reuse. People often pay high prices for old items.

Chimney pots removed from old houses before they were pulled down are stored for reuse.

Creating Less Waste

We can all cut down on the amount of waste we produce and save energy and materials. Collect and separate newspapers, bottles, cans and plastics that can be recycled.

Most of our rubbish is packaging, so buy goods which use little or no packaging. Reuse empty containers for other things, and pass on old clothes and toys for other people to use.

In a market in China, used cardboard boxes are collected for recycling.

A fruit stall in Cairo, Egypt. In markets, items are usually sold 'loose' and wrapped only in paper bags. This creates less waste packaging.

Recycling Topic Web

Maths
Collect, record and interpret data arising from a 'litter survey'.
Sorting into groups.

Art
Junk models.
Design a poster or logo to encourage recycling.

P.E./Dance Drama
Role play a refuse collector.
Move like machines that crush/dispose of rubbish.

Geography
Visit the local recycling centre.
Express views on attractive/unattractive features of local environment, for example, tidiness, noise.
How can quality be sustained and improved?

History
Look at photos and maps to see how the local environment has changed.
Investigate change in rubbish since 100 years ago (mainly ash from coal fires).

Recycling

Language
Share poems and stories with recycling as a theme, for example, *The Irn Man* by Ted Hughes or *Charlie's House* by Reviva Schermbuker.
Survey of local recycling bins – how many? location? are there enough? are they well designed?

Music
Sing songs with litter or recycling as a theme.
Make musical instruments using junk and compose a piece of music.

R.E.
What do charities do?
Collecting and selling things for charity.

Technology
Making meals with foods such as potatoes, nuts, seeds.
Cookery.
Making playthings with food packaging.

Science
Sort 'clean' litter into groups - plastic, paper, metal, and so on.
Explore and recognize similarities and differences between materials.
What do we throw away at home/school? Can any be recycled?
Recycling in nature – leaf litter, beetles, and so on.

Glossary

Aluminium A light, silvery metal which is dug out of the ground as bauxite.

Cellophane paper Thin but strong see-through paper.

Charity shop A shop which collects and sells second-hand things and gives the money to an organization which helps people in need.

Incinerator A furnace or fire for burning rubbish.

Landfill site A huge hole in the ground into which crushed rubbish is tipped. When the hole is filled, the site is covered with grass or used for new buildings.

Magnet A piece of iron which has been magnetized so that it can attract steel and other pieces of iron.

Material Stuff that something is made of – wood, plastic, paper, glass are all materials.

Oil A black liquid which takes millions of years to form underground. Plastic is made from oil, and oil is burned in power stations to make electricity.

Packaging Container or wrapping that something is sold in.

Pollutes/pollution Dirty or harmful waste which damages the air, water or land.

Recycling centre The place where articles such as old newspapers, bottles, cans and plastic bottles are collected and separated, ready to be recycled.

Recycled/recycling When an object is recycled, the material it is made of is reprocessed to make something else.

Reused Used again.

Further Reading
Domestic Waste by Tony Hare (Gloucester Press, 1992).
Glass by Hazel Songhurst; *Paper* by Andrew Langley; *Plastics* by Wayne Jackman (Wayland, 1996).
Reuse, Repair, Recycle by Jan McHarry (Gaia Books, 1993)
Rubbish by Sally Morgan (Wayland, 1993).
Rubbish and Recycling by Rosie Harlow and Sally Morgan, (Kingfisher, 1995).

Index